The Over-the-Top Histories of Chew the Scenery
and Other Idioms

by Arnold Ringstad • illustrated by Dan McGeehan

Published by The Child's World®
1980 Lookout Drive • Mankato, MN 56003-1705
800-599-READ • www.childsworld.com

Acknowledgments
The Child's World®: Mary Berendes, Publishing Director
The Design Lab: Design and production
Red Line Editorial: Editorial direction

Design elements: Kirsty Pargeter/iStockphoto

Copyright © 2013 by The Child's World®
All rights reserved. No part of this book may be reproduced or utilized in any form or by any means without written permission from the publisher.

ISBN 9781614732341
LCCN 2012932812

Printed in the United States of America
Mankato, MN
July 2012
PA02118

Contents

Blow off steam, 4
Pull the plug, 5
Spelling bee, 6
Eat crow, 7
Tongue-in-cheek, 8
Right off the bat, 9
In the nick of time, 10
Upper crust, 11
Red herring, 12
Get your goat, 13
Frog in your throat, 14
A chip off the old block, 15
Chew the scenery, 16
Apple of your eye, 17
On cloud nine, 18
Wrong side of the tracks, 19
Spill the beans, 20
Davy Jones' locker, 21
Stiff upper lip, 22
Tip of the iceberg, 23
Foot the bill, 24
Beyond the pale, 25
Yellow journalism, 26
Gravy train, 27
Butterfingers, 28
Two cents, 29
Cream of the crop, 30
Hit pay dirt, 31
About the author and illustrator, 32

BLOW OFF STEAM

MEANING: When you **blow off steam**, you relieve stress or energy by doing or saying something.

ORIGIN: Steam engines build up pressure. Some steam has to be released to prevent them from exploding.

EXAMPLE: Ming liked to **blow off steam** by playing kickball with his friends.

PULL THE PLUG

MEANING: When you **pull the plug** on something, you stop or end it.

ORIGIN: This phrase refers to drains in sinks or tubs. When you pull the plug, all the water drains out.

EXAMPLE: Josh decided to **pull the plug** on his science fair project. He noticed that three other people were doing the same experiment.

SPELLING BEE

MEANING: A **spelling bee** is a contest in which children compete by spelling words.

ORIGIN: Community farm activities were once called bees. This later expanded to any community activity, and was first used for spelling contests in the late 1800s.

EXAMPLE: Fifth-grader Jamie won the **spelling bee** against eighth graders.

EAT CROW

MEANING: To **eat crow** is to be ashamed by admitting an error.

ORIGIN: This idiom compares the unpleasantness of being ashamed to the unpleasantness of actually eating a crow.

EXAMPLE: Jerome had to **eat crow** after forgetting his brother's birthday.

TONGUE-IN-CHEEK

MEANING: When you say something **tongue-in-cheek**, you are saying it not to be taken seriously.

ORIGIN: Pressing your tongue against your cheek can cause you to wink, showing that you are not being serious. Putting your tongue in your cheek can also stop you from laughing at what you are saying.

EXAMPLE: When he said he could run faster than a cheetah, Dave was saying it **tongue-in-cheek**.

RIGHT OFF THE BAT

MEANING: Something that happens **right off the bat** happens right away.

ORIGIN: This phrase comes from baseball. It refers to the high speed at which a ball travels after a batter hits it.

EXAMPLE: Mila knew she would like her new teacher **right off the bat**.

IN THE NICK OF TIME

MEANING: Something that happens **in the nick of time** happens at just the right moment.

ORIGIN: A nick is a mark in a particular place. Something that happens in the nick of time happens at a particular time.

EXAMPLE: Jennifer got to school **in the nick of time** before it started raining.

UPPER CRUST

MEANING: A person in the **upper crust** is in a high social class.

ORIGIN: Originally, this phrase was used to talk about the actual crust of the earth. Later it came to mean a person's head, and finally simply something that was on top. From this meaning, it became a derogatory phrase for upper-class people.

EXAMPLE: Ira figured that most people on TV were in the **upper crust**.

RED HERRING

MEANING: A **red herring** is a misleading or fake clue.

ORIGIN: This phrase comes from the use of red herring fish to train foxhunting dogs. The dogs would have to learn how to tell the herrings apart from foxes.

EXAMPLE: The detective found nothing but **red herrings** for most of the movie.

GET YOUR GOAT

MEANING: Something that **gets your goat** makes you angry.

ORIGIN: The origin of this idiom is unclear. It was first used in the United States in the early 1900s. At that time, *goat* may have been a slang term meaning "anger."

EXAMPLE: It always **got Pedro's goat** when his pen ran out of ink in the middle of a test.

FROG IN YOUR THROAT

MEANING: When your throat is hoarse, you have a **frog in your throat**.

ORIGIN: A person whose throat is hoarse might sound as though they are croaking like a frog. The earliest known use of the phrase was in the late 1800s. It came from an advertisement for medicine used to cure hoarseness.

EXAMPLE: Kim had a **frog in her throat**. She wouldn't be able to sing in choir.

A CHIP OFF THE OLD BLOCK

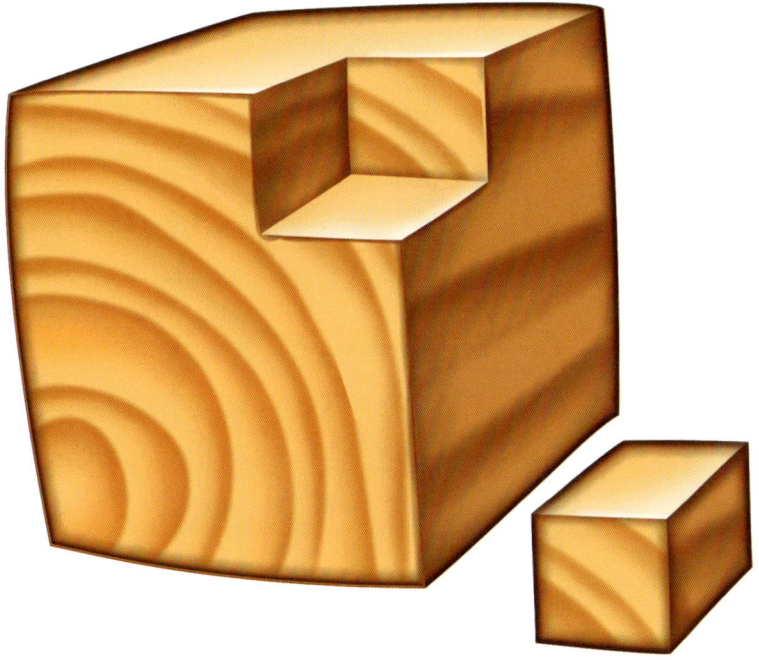

MEANING: When something looks like its source, it is **a chip off the old block**. The phrase is often used when a person looks like his or her parents.

ORIGIN: This phrase comes from woodworking. A chip off a block of wood would look very similar to the original block. The phrase has been used since at least the 1600s.

EXAMPLE: Mo always wore the same kind of hat as his father. He really was **a chip off the old block**.

CHEW THE SCENERY

MEANING: An actor who **chews the scenery** is acting very dramatically.

ORIGIN: This phrase comes from the idea that if an actor is overdramatic, they might as well be chewing the actual scenery onstage.

EXAMPLE: The audience groaned when the movie actor started **chewing the scenery**.

APPLE OF YOUR EYE

MEANING: If a person is important or precious to you, they are the **apple of your eye**.

ORIGIN: The pupil of the eye was once also called the apple. This phrase came about because eyes and eyesight are precious.

EXAMPLE: Roger's baby sister was the **apple of his eye**.

ON CLOUD NINE

MEANING: When you are **on cloud nine**, you are extremely happy.

ORIGIN: There have been many phrases with numbered clouds that have the same meaning. Cloud seven, cloud eight, and even cloud thirty-nine have been used. Cloud nine became the most popular version in the 1980s. The "cloud" part may refer to a happy feeling of floating.

EXAMPLE: Malia was **on cloud nine** after winning a giant stuffed animal at the carnival.

WRONG SIDE OF THE TRACKS

MEANING: A person who lives on the **wrong side of the tracks** lives on the bad side of town.

ORIGIN: The origin of this idiom is uncertain. It may come from towns that are split in half by a railroad track. The winds would carry soot and smoke from the train to one side more than the other. That side would become dirtier and less desirable to live in.

EXAMPLE: Catherine always found books more interesting when the main character lived on the **wrong side of the tracks**.

SPILL THE BEANS

MEANING: When you **spill the beans**, you tell a secret.

ORIGIN: This phrase uses an older meaning of the word *spill*, meaning to give away a secret. *Beans* is just one of many words used along with *spill*.

EXAMPLE: Olivia **spilled the beans**. Her friend's surprise party would not be a surprise any more.

DAVY JONES' LOCKER

MEANING: The bottom of the sea is **Davy Jones' locker**.

ORIGIN: There are many theories about the origin of this idiom. One says that a pirate named Davy Jones would make people walk the plank and drown in the sea.

EXAMPLE: Howard accidentally dropped his phone off the side of the cruise ship. Now it was in **Davy Jones' locker**.

STIFF UPPER LIP

MEANING: A person who has a **stiff upper lip** is courageous in a difficult situation.

ORIGIN: This comes from the way a person's upper lip trembles when they begin crying. Keeping the lip stiff shows that you aren't crying. The phrase is commonly considered British, but it actually came from the United States.

EXAMPLE: Mohamed kept a **stiff upper lip** even when his football team was losing 56 to 0.

TIP OF THE ICEBERG

MEANING: When something is the **tip of the iceberg**, there is more to it than you can see on the surface.

ORIGIN: Usually, only a small part of an iceberg sticks out above the water, while most of it lies hidden beneath the surface.

EXAMPLE: Isabella finished her math problem set, but it was only the **tip of the iceberg**. She had a lot more homework.

FOOT THE BILL

MEANING: When you pay for something, you **foot the bill**.

ORIGIN: This phrase comes from the use of the word *foot* to mean the bottom of a bill, where the total is written. By the early 1800s, this was extended to mean actually paying the bill.

EXAMPLE: Since it was her friend's birthday, Anya decided to **foot the bill** for their movie tickets.

BEYOND THE PALE

MEANING: When you do something **beyond the pale**, you do something that is inappropriate.

ORIGIN: This idiom doesn't have anything to do with a lack of color. Instead, *pale* comes from the same source as *pole*, something you would build a fence with. Beyond the pale is beyond a boundary.

EXAMPLE: Kayla thought the pop star's new music video was **beyond the pale**.

YELLOW JOURNALISM

MEANING: Exaggerated and made-up journalism is **yellow journalism**.

ORIGIN: This idiom comes from a major newspaper rivalry from the late 1800s. The newspapers competed to present sensational news. The word *yellow* comes from a comic strip in one of the papers called *The Yellow Kid*.

EXAMPLE: Carl tried to keep **yellow journalism** out of his school newspaper.

GRAVY TRAIN

MEANING: A **gravy train** is a way to make money easily.

ORIGIN: The word *gravy* has been used to mean something that is easy to do. It is unclear how the word *train* was added to the phrase. It may be a reference to hoboes who would catch free rides on trains.

EXAMPLE: Sasha was on the **gravy train** now. Her new babysitting job paid twice as much as her old one.

BUTTERFINGERS

MEANING: If someone has **butterfingers**, they drop things frequently.

ORIGIN: This phrase refers to how slippery your fingers would be if they had butter on them.

EXAMPLE: After Earl dropped the football for the third time in a row, his friends all said he had **butterfingers**.

TWO CENTS

MEANING: A person's opinion is his or her **two cents**.

ORIGIN: This phrase came from England as "two pence," using English money. It is unclear where it came from before that. One possibility is that it was the money a player had to put in to play a card game.

EXAMPLE: Leonard always gave his **two cents** in his history class, even when no one asked him to.

CREAM OF THE CROP

MEANING: Something that is the **cream of the crop** is the very best.

ORIGIN: This phrase uses the idea that the cream is the best part of the milk. In fresh milk, cream rises to the top. The phrase was probably a slightly changed translation of the French phrase *crème de la crème*.

EXAMPLE: When it came to shoes, Quinn always picked the **cream of the crop**.

HIT PAY DIRT

MEANING: When you **hit pay dirt**, you find something valuable.

ORIGIN: This phrase comes from mining. When the miner found valuable ores and minerals in the dirt, he would get paid.

EXAMPLE: Hank spent three hours at the library before he **hit pay dirt**. He found the perfect book to use in his report.

About the Author

Arnold Ringstad lives in Minneapolis, where he graduated from the University of Minnesota in 2011. He enjoys reading books about space exploration and playing board games with his girlfriend. Writing about idioms makes him as happy as a clam.

About the Illustrator

Dan McGeehan loves being an illustrator. His art appears in many magazines and children's books. He currently lives in Oklahoma.

Edison Twp. Free Public Library
340 Plainfield Ave.
Edison, New Jersey 08817